An American Bird Conservancy
Compact Guide

Paul Lehman
Ornithological Editor

The American Bird Conservancy (ABC) is a U.S.-based, not-for-profit organization formed to unify bird conservation efforts across the Americas and dedicated to the conservation of birds throughout the Western Hemisphere. ABC practices conservation through partnership, bringing together the partners whose expertise and resources are best suited to each task.

The ABC Policy Council has a membership of more than 70 organizations sharing a common interest in the conservation of birds. Composed of ornithologists, policy specialists, educators, and general bird enthusiasts, the Council is a professional forum for exchanging information and discussing critical and emerging bird conservation issues. The Council provides policy and scientific advice to conservationists, stimulates a network of support for conservation policies through national, state, and local groups, and directly accomplishes conservation through ABC.

ABC is a working member of Partners in Flight (PIF), an Americas-wide coalition of more than 150 organizations and government agencies dedicated to bird conservation. Initially begun to find ways to reverse the decline in neotropical migratory bird species, PIF has broadened its scope to include all non-game birds in the Americas. PIF links birders, hunters, government, industry, landowners, and other citizens in a unified effort to conserve bird populations and habitats.

Many North American "birds" found in this guide spend more than half their lives in Latin America and the Caribbean. The needs for bird conservation in this region are at least as great as in the U.S. Through PIF, ABC is building U.S. support for capable, but often underfunded, conservation partners throughout the Americas.

PIF's bird conservation strategy, called the Flight Plan, can be obtained from ABC, the National Fish and Wildlife Foundation, or the U.S. Fish and Wildlife Service. PIF's National Coordinator serves on ABC's staff, and ABC helps implement the Flight Plan through its Important Bird Areas (IBA) initiative. ABC members receive *Bird Conservation*, the magazine about PIF and American bird conservation.

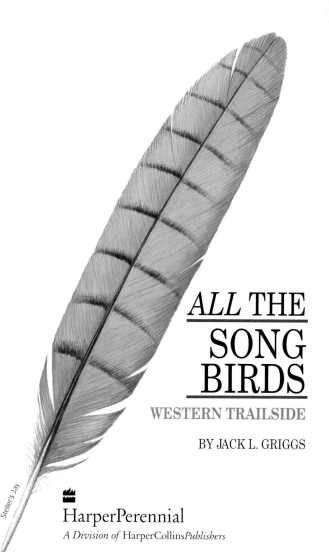

Steller's Jay

ALL THE
SONG
BIRDS

WESTERN TRAILSIDE

BY JACK L. GRIGGS

HarperPerennial

A Division of HarperCollins*Publishers*

Designed by Jack L. Griggs & Peg Alrich

Edited by Virginia Croft

Illustrations reformatted by John E. Griggs
from the original illustrations published in
All the Birds of North America
by the following artists:

F. P. Bennett pp. 29-31; John Dawson
pp. 43-63, center 65, 101-103; Dale Dyer
pp. 105-119; Larry McQueen pp. 81-99; Hans Peeters
pp. 65, 67-79; Doug Pratt pp. 33-41; Andrew Vallely pp. 25-27.

HarperCollins books may be purchased for educational, business, or sales
promotional use. For information, please write: Special Markets Department,
HarperCollins Publishers Inc., 10 East 53rd Street, New York, NY 10022.

FIRST EDITION

Library of Congress Cataloging-in-Publication Data is available upon request

ISBN 0-06-273695-7

00 01 02 03 04 PE 5 4 3 2 1

CONTENTS

WESTERN WOODLAND HABITATS

IDENTIFYING TRAILSIDE SONGBIRDS

CHECKLIST AND INDEX

WESTERN WOOD-LAND HABITATS

by
TERRY RICH

Birds, like other life, have evolved with their habitats. Over generations, natural selection has genetically tuned them to the vegetation in which they live. Birds know the best places to hide their nests, the best sources and types of food, and the best ways and places to hide if danger threatens. Take a bird from its familiar surroundings, place it in a strange habitat, and chances are that it won't succeed.

Mountainous terrain over much of the West provides a great diversity of vegetation over relatively short distances because of changes in aspect and elevation. Generally, by going up a given mountain or by going from the south side to the north, you will encounter increasingly moist forest types. And with the change in vegetation there is a corresponding change in birds to be found.

From a single point, for example, you can see lazuli buntings in streamside cottonwoods, plumbeous vireos in junipers on the adjacent south slope, and white-headed woodpeckers in ponderosa pines on the northern slope. And from the same point, Swainson's thrush can be heard singing in spruce-fir forests and MacGillivray's warbler in alder thickets slightly higher up the mountainside. These species are not limited to a single type of forest, but they may be numerous in their preferred habitat and scarce or rare in others.

Wildfire plays a critical role in forest health and bird habitat. About half of Yellowstone National Park burned in the summer of 1988 in what was viewed at the time as a major disaster. However, the results have proved not only that fire is a normal occurrence in western woodlands but that it is essential. The long-term value of a burn far outweighs the short-term negative effects.

Usually many dead trees are left standing or on the ground after a forest fire. A forest of dead trees is every bit as valuable for kestrels, western bluebirds, mountain chickadees, and many woodpeckers as is a forest of live trees. The Yellowstone fire provided much-needed habitat that had been dwindling out of natural balance for decades because of human fire suppression.

DEAD TREES AFTER A BURN

A succession of plant life occurs after a wildfire (or some other disaster, such as an avalanche, insect infestation, logging, or wind storm). Typically, the first vegetation includes forbs and grasses. Shrubs and small trees then proliferate. When trees become large but not so crowded as to block the sky, the forest is considered to be open canopy. Eventually the canopy closes on most forests, and finally, as trees age and continue to grow, the forest returns to old growth.

Most birds prefer a specific stage in succession more than others, and some are very particular. The spotted towhee, for instance, prefers the shrubby stage and will tolerate only a few scattered trees. Bluebirds will nest in second growth as long as some open canopy remains. Varied thrushes and winter wrens live in the dark, damp lower story of closed forest.

Individual birds must find a new home when their old one disappears through burn or forest succession. Some, perhaps most, species simply will not nest if they can't find habitat that meets their requirements. Consequently, we must preserve large areas of native woodlands of all types and in various stages of succession. The wildlife that has evolved with them cannot just find another habitat.

An edge is created where wildfire stops. Forest edges also occur at interruptions such as streams, meadows, and rocky outcrops. Many birds find forest edges particularly attractive because they use the habitats on both sides of the edge or the diverse vegetation that marks the edge. The red-shafted flicker, for example, nests in tall trees but frequently feeds on the ground at the forest edge. Even the edge created by a trail will tend to attract birds and other wildlife.

Riparian woodlands — the narrow strip of lush vegetation that flanks streams, rivers, ponds, and springs — are the most productive forests. Riparian woods and other wetlands comprise less than one percent of western land, yet they support more species and numbers of birds than any other habitat type.

FREMONT COTTONWOOD LEAF

In much of the Southwest, yellow warblers, common yellowthroats, and numerous other songbirds are never far from the cottonwoods and willows of riparian woodlands. Go into a temperate rain forest on the west side of the Cascade Mountains in Washington or Oregon, however, and you can find songbirds over wide areas. For many of them, the damp woodlands of the West Cascades function like one large riparian area.

The vertical structure of riparian habitats is important. Some birds stick close to the ground in heavy understory vegetation; others spend most of their time in the canopy of tall trees. Most species are less demanding and may use various levels of vegetation.

Historically, cattle grazing, river damming, and water diversion have severely reduced and degraded riparian habitats. The best indicators of the condition of riparian habitats are those species that use the understory vegetation. When improper livestock grazing destroys the undergrowth, birds like Bewick's wren and Swainson's thrush disappear.

High in the mountains, riparian understory species include MacGillivray's warbler and Lincoln's sparrow. Along mountain streams, look for the amazing dipper — a plump, gray waterbird that forages for insects at the edges of and *under* the surface of cascading mountain waters. It is not a songbird and is not described in this book, but when hiking along mountain streams, keep an eye out for wren-like birds at the very edge of the water or flying up- or downstream.

DIPPER

Another group of birds is seen near the ground but also tends to move up to mid-story vegetation if it is available. The eye-dazzling lazuli bunting is in this group, which also includes such diverse birds as the veery and calliope hummingbird.

In the riparian canopy, usually out of sight and identified by song, are tanagers, orioles, and grosbeaks. The tall trees that provide canopy are typically cottonwoods but may include willow, sycamore, box elder, aspen, and alder, among others.

Majestic cottonwoods create some of the most beautiful gallery forests on the continent. Unfortunately, the cottonwood component has been lost in some riparian woodlands and continues to be lost in others because of dams that control water flow. In order for their seedlings to become established, cottonwoods require the flooding and scouring action of natural river fluctuations.

UTAH JUNIPER TWIG AND BERRIES

Juniper woodlands are widespread in western Colorado, Utah, Nevada, northern Arizona, and New Mexico. They are generally the lowest woodland on a mountain, just above the sagebrush zone, often in scattered patches on arid, rocky land. In many localities, piñon pines are mixed with junipers. Where junipers grow densely, the understory vegetation disappears because of shading, competition for scarce moisture, and growth-inhibiting chemicals released into the soil by the junipers.

PIÑON PINE CONE AND SEED

Wildfire is less of a threat without flammable understory, and as a result, junipers can reach very old ages — over 1,000 years is not uncommon. Old trees are especially likely to provide natural cavities for such species as the ash-throated flycatcher and juniper titmouse. Juniper woodlands are the only forests in the West that have expanded since the arrival of Europeans.

Pinyon jays and black-throated gray warblers are two of the species common in junipers. Townsend's solitaire winters almost exclusively in junipers, feeding on the berries. And little chipping sparrows, although they utilize diverse woodlands, are especially fond of the bare ground around junipers. Gray and plumbeous vireos share juniper woodlands, giving the observer the chance to compare the plumages and songs of these generally similar species.

Oak woodlands, like juniper woods, occur in relatively pure stands in California and Oregon and mixed with other non-oak species in southwestern Colorado and adjacent states. Western oaks include both deciduous and evergreen species. The evergreens keep their leaves year-round, providing both cover and foraging sites for birds.

**VALLEY OAK
(DECIDUOUS)**

The bounty of acorns produced by oaks attracts acorn specialists, including jays, woodpeckers, and the little oak titmouse. Perhaps the best-known specialist is the acorn woodpecker. These comical, noisy, social, and very attractive woodpeckers seem to be constantly on the move and are easily located if present.

**COAST LIVE OAK
(EVERGREEN)**

Flocks of band-tailed pigeons feed on acorns as well. Although not a songbird and not included in this guide, the band-tail can be easily recognized by its broad gray tail band, yellow feet, and black-tipped yellow bill. The smaller mourning doves have long pointed tails. City pigeons have a relatively narow black tail band and seldom occur in woodlands with band-tails.

AND-TAILED PIGEON

Numerous songbirds found in other forest types inhabit oak woodlands. Some of the most common are the bushtit and Bullock's oriole. Cassin's vireo and Hutton's vireo, like the plumbeous and gray vireos of juniper woodlands, are both found in oak woodlands and provide an excellent challenge for sharpening bird identification skills. They look different and sing differently, but the differences are subtle.

MOURNING DOVE

Ponderosa pine woodlands, which occur throughout the Rocky Mountains and Sierra Nevada, are now the rarest old-growth type in the West. They are a logger's favorite because they grow straight, they grow huge, and they generally grow at low elevations, where they are accessible. Relatively few huge trees still exist. For best growth, ponderosas need frequent low-intensity fires to burn the undergrowth and kill back smaller trees. As fires reduce the competition for nutrients, water, and sunlight, the existing big trees keep getting bigger.

13

Birds that prefer big, old ponderosas, such as the white-headed woodpecker, pygmy nuthatch, and white-breasted nuthatch, are greatly reduced in the Northwest. White-headed woodpeckers are beautiful western birds that depend heavily on pine seeds, which they extract by boring into the cones. The most common birds in ponderosa pines are generalists, such as pine siskins, flickers, wood-pewees, western bluebirds, and Audubon's (yellow-rumped) warblers.

PONDEROSA PINE NEEDLES

Lodgepole pines form vast expanses of forest in the Northern Rockies well into Canada and were the primary trees that went up in flames in the summer of 1998 in Yellowstone National Park. That fire demonstrated that we are not left with a permanently desolate, black hole in the earth after such an event. Immediately all sorts of things begin to grow — grass, flowers, little trees.

LODGEPOLE PINE NEEDLES

One of my young children, on walking through the Yellowstone burn in 1990, asked, "Dad, how do they make the grass so green?" The grass along the forest trail was particularly lush and green because it was soaking in nutrients and sunlight for the first time in hundreds of years. Birds that use open habitats, such as hummers and towhees, were abundant.

14

Some Yellowstone birds now using the post-burn vegetation will eventually disappear from these habitats, including the lazuli bunting, mountain bluebird, and robin. Both black-backed and three-toed woodpeckers foraged among the dead trees for insects for a few years but have become much less common as the insect infestations have dropped off.

It will be 200 to 300 years before the burned forests at Yellowstone mature again. Old lodgepole pine forests are wonderful places to be, but not for bird song — for their silence. Like the redwood forests of coastal California, these woodlands remind me of a great quiet library.

The few songbirds commonly found in mature lodgepole pine forests include hermit and Swainson's thrushes, gray jays, mountain chickadees, juncos, and red-breasted nuthatches. Among the most prized of the lodgepole birds is the three-toed woodpecker, a specialist in dead or dying trees.

Douglas fir forests vary considerably, depending on the moisture available. In the Rocky Mountains, they typically grow on the northern slopes of mountains that may have southern slopes covered only in grass and sagebrush. These relatively dry sites produce mature trees around 100 feet tall and 2 feet in diameter. They attract many of the same birds that use lodgepole pine woodlands.

DOUGLAS FIR CONE

But in the plentiful rainfall on the west side of the Cascades, Douglas firs look like another species. They become monsters up to 8 feet in diameter and may shoot 250 feet into the sky. In this moist setting, many other plants also grow, creating a much more complex woodland than seen in southern Idaho, for example.

The birds, too, are largely different. The big prize for most of us is the varied thrush. Fortunately, this beautiful cousin of the robin is not rare, but it is shy and may be a little difficult to find at times. Its eerie, ventriloquial song provides few clues to its location among the giant trees.

Common songbirds in damp Douglas firs include orange-crowned warblers, red cross-bills, and one of the finest singers in North America — the tiny winter wren. The magnificent pileated woodpecker is also numerous in Douglas firs and may be the only bird large enough to avoid looking like a toy in the old growth.

Woodlands of quaking aspen occur across western North America and provide a wonderful contrast in color and bird community to the many coniferous forest types in the West. Their delicate green in early spring, spectacular gold in autumn, and bare branches in the dead of winter may produce the only seasonal cues on slopes that are otherwise truly evergreen.

QUAKING ASPEN LEAF

Two features of the aspen are important to birds: the trees are relatively soft, and they are short-lived, providing plenty of places for nest cavities. Hole-nesting violet-green swallows may be the most common bird in an aspen grove. Other relatively easy to find hole-nesters include sapsuckers, hairy woodpeckers, house wrens, and mountain bluebirds.

I suspect there is at least one warbling vireo in every aspen patch in the West. This drab little bird may be difficult to see in the canopy of leaves, but its cheerful song may be the only one heard in the middle of a hot July afternoon.

ENGELMANN SPRUCE NEEDLES

Spruce and fir — typically Engelmann spruce and subalpine fir — comprise a large portion of many of our national parks and forests on the eastern slopes of the Cascades and in the Rockies. Spruce-fir forests are home to a host of the most common western songbirds and such prizes as the the golden-crowned kinglet, Clark's nutcracker, and the surprisingly tame pine grosbeak.

SUBALPINE FIR NEEDLES

In the Pacific Northwest, many more species of spruce and fir occur, often mixed with yet other conifers. These woodlands grow huge trees and include more complex vegetation that attracts species in addition to those birds found in the Rockies. These include the chestnut-backed chickadee and several warblers — Townsend's, hermit, Nashville, and the black-throated gray.

Across northern Canada and Alaska (but outside the range of the maps in this guide) are vast forest expanses that serve as breeding refuge for numerous songbirds seen only during migration over most of the US. Nearly all the birds seen in northern forests are illustrated in this guide, as they occur in the US and southern Canada as well. Only a few Arctic specialties, such as the boreal chickadee and Siberian tit, are missing.

At the northern limits, woodland structure is controlled more by subzero temperatures than by moisture. Because of the low angle of the sun at such high latitudes, the importance of slope is even greater in Canada than it is in Colorado, for example.

South-facing slopes in Alaska are warmer and drier and support more productive aspen and birch woodlands. North slopes often are poorly drained areas with cold, wet soils that support only miniature, Hobbit-like black spruce woodlands.

WHITE FIR NEEDLES

Most common among the northern forests are white spruce and paper birch woodlands, where birds like the gray jay, varied thrush, and three-toed woodpecker can be more common than they are in the Cascades or Rockies of the lower 48 states.

PAPER BIRCH CATKINS

Most productive of all the northern forests are the cottonwoods that grow along some northern rivers. The cottonwoods of Alaska attract many of the same birds as cottonwoods in Nevada, for instance. They also attract songbirds like Wilson's warbler, fox sparrows, and white-crowned sparrows, which usually nest in higher elevations (above the cottonwood zone) in much of the the rest of the US. Other birds, such as the brown creeper, dark-eyed junco, and Audubon's (yellow-rumped) warbler, that are typically seen in conifers in the lower 48 states can be found in Alaska's cottonwoods.

HOW TO LOOK AT A BIRD

The way birds feed and their adaptations for feeding are the most important points to recognize in identifying and understanding a bird. For the beginner, the color and pattern of an unknown bird can be so striking that important points of shape and behavior go unnoticed. But feeding adaptations, especially bill shape, best reveal a bird's role in nature — its truest identity.

Owls, hawks, doves, woodpeckers, and many other birds are easily recognized by shape and behavior. Songbirds are more confusing. If you don't immediately recognize a songbird as a sparrow, a wren, or a warbler, for example, try to see its bill shape. Is it a seed-crusher or a bug-eater? Seed-crushers have strong, conical bills for cracking seeds. The shape of a bug-eater's bill varies with the way it catches bugs.

conical bill

Most bug-eaters have slender, straight bills used to probe in trees, brush, ground litter, and rock crevices. A few have curved bills for specialized probing. And some, the fly-catcher group, have broad-based, flat bills. Flycatchers catch bugs in midair, and their broad bills improve their chances of success.

straight bill

curved bill

If bill shape can't be seen, a bird's feeding behavior is often just as revealing. Sparrows

flycatching bill

don't flit among the branches of a tree searching for bugs, and warblers won't be seen on the ground picking at seeds.

Knowing its bill shape or feeding behavior reduces the possible identities of an unknown songbird. Plumage marks can then be used to identify all the trailside songbirds.

Most names used to describe parts of a bird are predictable — back, crown, throat, etc. Three names that might not be immediately understood are rump, undertail coverts, and wing bars. The rump is at the base of the tail, topside; undertail coverts cover the base of the tail, bottomside. Wing bars are formed by the contrasting tips (often white) of the feathers that help cover the wing when it is folded.

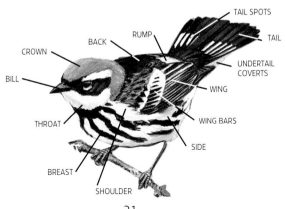

HOW TO READ THE MAPS

Range maps provide a simplified picture of a species' distribution. They indicate the birds that can be expected in any local region. Birds are not evenly distributed over their ranges. They require suitable habitat (no seeds, no sparrows) and are typically scarcest at their range limits. Some birds are numerous but not commonly seen because they are secretive.

Weather and food availability affect bird distribution in winter. Some birds regularly retreat to warmer southern weather or to the narrow coastal band where the Pacific moderates the worst of the winter. Other birds are adapted to successfully forage — a few even nest and raise their young — while enduring freezing winds and drifting snow.

MAP KEY

SUMMER OR NESTING

WINTER

ALL YEAR

MIGRATION
(spring & fall)

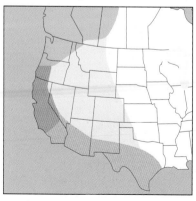

HOW THE BIRDS ARE ORGA-NIZED

Not all woodpeckers are called woodpeckers — flickers and sapsuckers, for instance, are also wood-peckers. In the list below, birds with names different from their common group name are listed in parentheses following the group name.

WHITE-THROATED SWIFT

VAUX'S SWIFT

Vaux's swift is closely related to the chimney swift in the East, which once roosted in hollow trees but has adapted almost completely to chimneys.

With the loss of mature forests with hollow nesting and roosting trees in the West, Vaux's is diminishing more than adapting.

Ever on the wing, swifts course the skies over woodlands collecting bugs. Only bad weather or darkness grounds them.

White-throated swifts are fairly numerous but very local, depending on traditional rocky cliffs to provide cracks and crevices for their nests. They find suitable cliffs in mountains, along the coast, and in desert canyons. Individuals and small groups forage widely over the surrounding terrain. Flying at speeds of over 200 mph, the white-throated swift is, indeed, swift; it could be North America's fastest-flying bird.

Vaux's swift depends on large hollow trees — dead or alive — for nesting and roosting. Some have adapted to chimneys. They are fairly numerous and spend most of their time feeding over coniferous or mixed forests, often congregating over lakes or watercourses at morning and evening or during heavy weather.

Swifts fly faster and more erratically than swallows. Their constant, jerky flight adjustments are different from the graceful, acrobatic flight of swallows and can create the illusion of alternating wing beats. The distinctive black-and-white pattern of the **white-throated swift** is a sure mark. **Vaux's swift** is a more even gray-brown with noticeably lighter areas on the throat and rump.

24

White-throated Swift

Vaux's Swift

SWALLOWS

ROUGH-WINGED SWALLOW

TREE SWALLOW

VIOLET-GREEN SWALLOW

Bank swallows, which nest at gravel pits and other steep banks, are brown above and white below with a brown breast band.

Swallows patrol the skies for flying insects, although the tree swallow supplements its bug diet with berries. Tree and violet-green swallows nest in tree hollows, but none of the swallows are tightly associated with woodlands. Their primary associations are with bug-rich skies and the wet areas that typically produce them. Woodlands often border the wetlands.

The rough-winged swallow is adept at flying just above the terrain, especially water, and will sometimes follow small streams through woodlands. The "dirty" throat and breast of the **rough-winged swallow** distinguish it from young brown-and-white tree and violet-green swallows. Rough-winged swallows are fairly numerous, occurring singly and in small groups.

Violet-green swallows are numerous, and tree swallows are abundant. They feed in small groups, skimming the ground or sweeping overhead. The white on the **violet-green swallow** extends prominently from the underparts onto the rump and face. On the **tree swallow,** white is restricted to the underparts.

Note that swallows have a different wing shape than the similar swifts (p. 24). Swallows have a distinct bend in the forewing. In the swift, this bend or "wrist" is so close to the body that the wing curves evenly almost its entire length.

Rough-winged Swallow

Tree Swallow

young

young

Violet-green Swallow

T his illustration includes all hummers that show substantial amounts of rusty red color — the males of two species and the females of four. The metallic red throats of the males often look black. Only when light strikes at a favorable angle are the jewel-like reflections visible. Females lack the brilliant throats; their flash of color is in the underside of their tails.

RUFOUS HUMMINGBIRD

ALLEN'S HUMMINGBIRD

Hummingbirds take small insects, as well as flower nectar.

Nesting ranges of **Allen's** and **rufous hummingbirds** are almost totally separate. During migration, the male Allen's green back separates it from the male rufous hummer, which can show a few flecks of green on its rufous back. Rufous hummers are numerous, attending flowers from mountain meadows to lowland gardens. Allen's are less numerous but common in the coastal regions of California.

Female rufous and Allen's hummingbirds are inseparable in the field, and distinguishing either from female broad-tailed and calliope hummers requires a good view. **Female broad-tailed hummingbirds** are larger than the female rufous or Allen's, with a bulkier tail and a slightly different tail pattern. **Female calliope hummingbirds** are smaller than rufous or Allen's and have short tails with little or no rufous color evident. When the bird perches, its folded wings reach beyond the tail tip.

♀ broad-tailed
p. 30

**Rufous
Hummingbird**

♀ rufous & Allen's

**Allen's
Hummingbird**

♀ calliope
p. 30

CALLIOPE HUMMINGBIRD

ANNA'S HUMMINGBIRD

BROAD-TAILED HUMMINGBIRD

BLACK-CHINNED HUMMINGBIRD

The green-sided hummers include four males and two females. All the males have distinctive iridescent throats.

The calliope hummer, North America's smallest nesting bird, weighs about as much as a penny and is barely 3 inches long, bill included. It is fairly numerous in mountain meadows and forest clearings, especially near streams. The small size and burst of red rays on the throat of the **male calliope** are good marks.

Anna's hummingbird is bulky — at least by hummingbird standards. Males have a rose-red crown and throat. Females are dirty gray below. They are often seen in gardens and parks feeding from cultivated plants. On the Pacific slope of California, Anna's is fairly numerous in chaparral and open woodlands.

At high elevations in the southern Rocky Mountains, the broad-tailed hummer frequents flowers in forest glades. It is fairly numerous. One of the best marks for the **male broad-tailed hummer** is the loud trill its wings make.

Black-chinned hummers are fairly numerous, especially at lower elevations. The violet throat band is an important mark for the male, as the throats of other male hummers can often appear black. The female's white underparts can have a hint of buff — no more — on the flanks.

Calliope
Hummingbird

♀ black-chinned

Anna's
Hummingbird

♀ Anna's

Broad-tailed
Hummingbird

Black-chinned
Hummingbird

PILEATED & FLICKER

PILEATED WOODPECKER

RED-SHAFTED FLICKER

Gilded flickers, with yellow rather than red wing linings, are found in parts of Arizona and nearby California.

Lewis' Woodpecker is scarce and scattered throughout the West. In summer, it is often seen in mountain stands of ponderosa pines. It has a greenish back, gray collar, pink belly, and red face.

Because of their size, pileated woodpeckers need large trees for nesting and roosting. Look for them in mature forests, and also in younger woods with scattered large dead trees. They feed on ants and beetle larvae in live and decaying wood. Nuts and berries are taken seasonally.

A crow-sized bird, the **pileated woodpecker** is quite distinctive and not likely to be confused with crows or other woodpeckers. Note the red moustache mark on the male. A loud drumming or a *wuk-wuk-wuk-wuk* call is often heard before the bird is seen.

Flickers are woodpeckers. The red-shafted flicker is the form of the northern flicker seen in the West. It is numerous and often seen foraging for ants on the ground in open woodlands or at forest edges. The plumage is unmistakable with a good look, but the birds are shy and often fly off at a distance. Because they often take off from the ground, red-shafted flickers are sometimes not recognized as woodpeckers by those unfamiliar with them.

As a **red-shafted flicker** flies off, the white rump patch and flash of red in the wings are good, easily seen marks. At close range, females can be seen to lack the red mustache mark of the male.

Pileated Woodpecker

Red-shafted Flicker

WOOD-PECKERS

DOWNY
WOODPECKER

HAIRY
WOODPECKER

Black-backed and three-toed woodpeckers are scarce birds found in newly dead conifers. They are darker than hairy woodpeckers, with black barring on their white sides, and lack white wing spots. The back is black or (in the three-toed) barred black and white. Males have gold crown patches.

The most common woodpecker along most western trails is the little downy. The hairy woodpecker has virtually the identical plumage pattern but is larger. In parts of the West, both are dirty gray rather than white. They are seen throughout western forests, feeding primarily on insects and larvae.

The difference in size of the hairy and downy is significant but can be hard to judge unless the birds are seen together, as sometimes happens at feeders. A better mark is bill length. The **hairy woodpecker** has a much larger bill — nearly as long as its head. The **downy woodpecker's** bill extends only about half its head length. The hairy also gives a noticeably sharper *peek!* call than the downy.

Males of both species have a bright red patch on the back of their crowns, lacking in females. Young birds (both sexes) also show a patch of red on their heads, but the color is more diffuse and is located on the center or forepart of the crown rather than on the rear.

There is a very small plumage difference that can be noted on birds at close range. The white outer tail feathers on the hairy woodpecker are usually unmarked, while those on the downy woodpecker have two or more black bars.

34

hairy

young

Downy
Woodpecker

♀

♂

♀

Hairy
Woodpecker

♂

WOOD-PECKERS

NUTTALL'S WOODPECKER

LADDER-BACKED WOODPECKER

ACORN WOODPECKER

White-headed woodpeckers are shy and scarce in mountain conifers of the coastal states. They are black overall, with a white face and wing patch.

Ladder-backed and Nuttall's woodpeckers are closely related neighbors, with ranges barely overlapping in southern California. The ladder-backed is numerous in southwestern woods, brush, and even cholla cactus. It forages on the ground and in shrubs, as well as on trees. Nuttall's is fairly numerous in California broad-leaved and mixed woodlands, especially among oaks, sycamores, and at streamside willows and cottonwoods.

The extensive black-and-white striping on their backs, wings, and heads is a good mark separating the ladder-backed and Nuttall's from other western woodpeckers. Males have a red crown patch. **Nuttall's woodpecker** is crisper black and white than the **ladder-backed woodpecker** and has a larger black area on the cheek and side of the neck.

Acorn woodpeckers are numerous in oak and pine-oak woodlands. They flycatch and pick acorns from the treetops, storing the nuts in holes drilled in a "granary" tree. Thousands of acorns are commonly stored in a single tree.

The striking head pattern of the **acorn woodpecker** is sufficient for identification. The whitish eye-rings give the birds a comical aspect. Acorn woodpeckers are often seen in small groups of up to a dozen individuals.

Nuttall's Woodpecker

♀

♂

Ladder-backed Woodpecker

♀

♂

♂

♀

Acorn Woodpecker

SAPSUCKERS

WILLIAMSON'S SAPSUCKER

RED-BREASTED SAPSUCKER

RED-NAPED SAPSUCKER

Sapsucker wells are also visited by some hummers and warblers. The holes don't harm the tree but do show up on the sawn wood, decreasing its commercial value.

Sapsuckers are woodpeckers with a specialized foraging strategy. They drill neat rows of small holes in selected trees and then return to drink the sap that collects. The sap wells also attract bugs, ants in particular, and the sapsucker consumes them just as readily.

Williamson's sapsuckers are uncommon. They summer in mountain conifers and winter at lower elevations, primarily in pine–oak and oak–juniper woodlands. The male **Williamson's sapsucker** has the broad white stripe on the wing characteristic of sapsuckers; females wear a finely striped brown plumage that is very uncharacteristic for woodpeckers of any type. The yellow belly is a good mark for both male and female.

Red-breasted and red-naped sapsuckers prefer mixed forests, especially with aspens, and are often seen in the mountains during summer. They drill their wells on hundreds of different kinds of trees.

The bold and distinctive head pattern of the **red-naped sapsucker** varies a bit with sex. Females have a white chin. The entire head and breast are red on the **red-breasted sapsucker.** The whitish streak on the face is longer in southern birds, and the red on the head and breast is less intense.

38

Williamson's Sapsucker

♀

♂

southern form

Red-breasted Sapsucker

northern form

Red-naped Sapsucker

♀

♂

WHITE-BREASTED NUTHATCH

RED-BREASTED NUTHATCH

BROWN CREEPER

The pygmy nuthatch is fairly numerous in mountain pines, especially ponderosa. The size of a red-breasted nuthatch, it is white below, with a creamy breast and dark cap.

uthatches and the brown creeper cling to the sides of trees like woodpeckers, searching for insects and larvae hidden in bark. Nuthatches are the only birds so agile that they can creep down a tree. Presumably, they find morsels that upward-climbers miss.

The **white-breasted nuthatch** is numerous. They are most common in open deciduous and mixed woodlands but can be found on any large tree. Some females are noticeably grayer on the crown than males. There is an inconspicuous wash of rusty red on the flanks.

Red-breasted nuthatches prefer conifers. Like the white-breasted, they are seen on tree trunks and large limbs but also forage for insects at the tips of small branches and take seeds from pine cones. They are numerous in western mountains, sometimes venturing in fall and winter into lowland woodlands. Smaller than the white-breasted nuthatch, they have rusty red underparts and a black eye stripe. Females are duller than males.

The **brown creeper** is fairly numerous in mature forests but often overlooked because it is quiet and blends in well with the tree trunks it frequents. It spirals up a large trunk inconspicuously and is often first noticed when it flies from one tree trunk to the base of another.

White-breasted
Nuthatch

♀

Red-
breasted
Nuthatch

♂

Brown Creeper

CEDAR WAXWING

LOGGERHEAD SHRIKE

Bohemian waxwings are fairly numerous in winter in the northern half of the western US, sometimes seen in flocks of cedar waxwings. The Bohemian is larger than the cedar waxwing. It has a gray belly, rusty undertail, and slightly different wing markings.

Waxwings nest in open woodlands. During the summer, they feed heavily on insects and are often seen near water where insects abound. Over the rest of the year, they wander in flocks of up to a hundred birds or so, searching for sugar-rich fruits (cedar berries are a favorite) as they come into season. Flocks keep in close contact with pleasing high-pitched, lisping calls.

The small dots of red on the wings of the **cedar waxwing** suggest the wax once used for sealing documents and are the source of the bird's name. The crest, narrow black mask, and yellow tail tip are easy identifying marks. Their upright posture and fastidiously smooth plumage give waxwings a military bearing.

Loggerhead shrikes are patterned much like the lankier mockingbird, but note the black mask, big head, and compact body. Young loggerhead shrikes have fine dark barring on their breasts and backs until fall.

Shrikes hunt alone over open country and nest in shrubs and scattered trees. Like the waxwing, they feed heavily on flying insects in summer, and both birds have broad-based bills like those of flycatchers. When the insect population collapses in fall, shrikes depend on a diet of small animals, including songbirds.

42

Cedar Waxwing

young

Loggerhead Shrike

shrike

mockingbird
p. 64

KINGBIRDS

Kingbirds usually perch conspicuously when not on flycatching forays. They are known for their aggressive, noisy attacks on other birds — and even people — who enter their defended territory.

CASSIN'S KINGBIRD

WESTERN KINGBIRD

Cassin's and the western kingbird look much alike and have much range in common, but they have somewhat different habitat preferences. Cassin's is fairly numerous in woodlands, from open woods to crowded forest with a fairly closed canopy, often at middle elevations.

The western kingbird is a bird of lower elevations and mountain valleys. It is numerous at woodland edges but prefers more open areas than does Cassin's. It needs only an occasional tree for perching or nesting. The planting of trees (and utility poles) in open areas has increased the western kingbird's range.

When kingbirds raise their crests in aggressive display, a few red feathers can sometimes be seen on the crown.

Both kingbirds bear a resemblance to the ash-throated flycatcher (p. 46) but lack its rusty wing and tail color. The head patterns are different also; kingbirds have white throats and gray crowns. **Cassin's kingbird** is darker gray than the **western kingbird,** making the white throat prominent. It is the dark gray mask that seems more prominent on the paler western kingbird. The white webs on the outer tail feathers of the western are usually easy marks.

Cassin's Kingbird

Western Kingbird

ASH-THROATED FLYCATCHER

EASTERN KINGBIRD

Brown-crested flycatchers are fairly numerous in dry woods of southern Arizona and South Texas. A little larger than the ash-throated, it is best identified by its *whit!* call. The underside of the tail is also distinctive.

Dusky-capped flycatchers of southern Arizona have brown tails and are a little smaller than ash-throateds.

Ash-throated flycatchers are widespread and fairly numerous in open woodlands and dry scrub. They aren't as aggressive as kingbirds but will occasionally harass a hawk or crow. Two close relatives that look very similar, the brown-crested flycatcher and dusky-capped flycatcher, are found in portions of the Southwest (see sidebar).

The rusty flash in the wings and tail is obvious when the **ash-throated flycatcher** is in flight. The underparts are very pale, with the ashy throat color extending onto the upper breast. The crown usually appears peaked or crested and is brown, contrasting with the ash-gray lower face and throat.

Despite its name, the eastern kingbird is numerous in the West. (It is actually declining in the East.) It inhabits a variety of open lands and woodland edges, usually flycatching from the top of shrubs or fences. In late summer and fall, it eats many berries, as well as bugs.

For a bird that is black and white, the **eastern kingbird** is quite attractive. The white tail tip is a sure mark. Males typically sit more erect than females and raise the feathers on their crown to maintain a slight crest. Agitated females posture like males, but females typically sit less erect and are rounder-headed, as illustrated.

Dusky-capped
Flycatcher

ash-
throated

brown-
crested

Ash-throated
Flycatcher

Eastern Kingbird

OLIVE-SIDED
FLYCATCHER

WESTERN
WOOD-PEWEE

EMPIDONAX
FLYCATCHERS

The gray flycatcher is an empidonax of semiarid lands that can be recognized by its habit of dipping its tail down slowly, then raising it.

Flycatchers, including pewees, typically sit on an exposed perch and wait for an insect to pass by. It is their patient waiting that is often the first clue to their identity. Most songbirds busily search the forest for insects; flycatchers sit and search the sky.

After a foray for an insect, flycatchers may return to the same perch. The **olive-sided flycatcher** returns almost inevitably to the same dead snag. It is fairly numerous in cool coniferous forests, often near water. It is larger than the other drab flycatchers and is also distinguished by its vest-like gray sides.

Pewees are numerous and widespread in western conifers and hardwoods. They often flycatch at clearings and alongside streams.

There are nine empidonax flycatchers in western woodlands, and they look much alike. Some are a little yellower below and greener above than others, but variation can be due more to plumage wear than species differences. Separating species is for experts.

Empids and pewees are often confused but can be reliably separated with a good look. **Empidonax flycatchers** have wing bars and eye-rings; they often flick their tails, especially on landing. **Western wood-pewees** have wing bars, no eye-rings, and don't flick their tails.

48

Olive-sided Flycatcher

Western Wood-Pewee

Empidonax Flycatchers

typical fresh fall plumage

typical worn summer plumage

SMALL FLYCATCHERS

BLACK PHOEBE

VERMILION FLYCATCHER

lack phoebes and vermilion flycatchers are both prevalent around water. The phoebe is rarely out of sight of water, be it a river, rain puddle, cattle tank, or the ocean. The willows, cottonwoods, and mesquites that border southwestern streams are favorite haunts for both birds.

Both birds flycatch from a low limb, post, or wire, seldom more than a few feet from the ground. Vermilion flycatchers often drop to the ground to catch an insect and then return quickly to a low perch.

Black phoebes look something like juncos (p. 112) but their behavior is all flycatcher. Young birds are a little browner than adults and have tawny wing bars. Black phoebes also have the distinctive habit of pumping their tails up and down. Vermilion flycatchers share this habit, but do so much less frequently.

Tail-pumping is a totally unnecessary mark for the brilliant adult male **vermilion flycatcher,** but it is a helpful mark for the female and young birds. Most females have a salmon or yellowish wash on the belly, but some young birds have none. A dark mask through the eyes is usually obvious on all individuals. It takes several years for males to attain their brightest plumage; yearlings can be paler, yellowish.

Black Phoebe

Vermilion Flycatcher

♀

young ♂

♂

CANYON WREN

ROCK WREN

CALIFORNIA THRASHER

Yellow-billed cuckoos are rare in most of the West, usually found in streamside trees. The size of a thrasher, they have white underparts and large white spots on their undertails.

Rocks provide shelter, nest sites, and hidden insects for both canyon and rock wrens. The rocky outcrops, boulder piles, and cliffs they inhabit can be in woodlands, grasslands, desert, or chaparral. The canyon wren is most common in shaded semiarid canyons or desert washes with steep, rocky outcrops. Rock wrens are less selective of their rock piles. Both species are fairly numerous, and their territories often overlap.

The bright, white throat and rusty underparts of the **canyon wren** easily distinguish it from the **rock wren.** Both wrens have black-barred tails, but the canyon wren's is rusty, not brown, and lacks the buff corners of the rock wren's tail. Both birds have a loud song, with the canyon wren giving a particularly pleasing cascade of sweet notes.

The California thrasher is the only one of several similar species that is commonly seen in woodlands. The others prefer open semiarid lands. Chaparral is the California thrasher's principal habitat, but it also lives in adjacent brushy woodlands. It uses its feet and long curved bill to noisily rake the ground for insects. A shy bird, it often remains hidden in brush. When surprised in the open, it usually runs to safety. The distinctive bill and brown plumage are easy marks for the **California thrasher.**

Canyon Wren

scale x1.5 to match
wrens on p. 55

Rock Wren

California Thrasher

WRENS

WINTER WREN

HOUSE WREN

BEWICK'S WREN

Wrens are small, energetic bug-eaters. Winter, house, and Bewick's wrens are usually seen in shrubs and dense underbrush on or near the ground. Although shy, they are loquacious and often located by the noisy scolding given when approached too closely.

Winter wrens are numerous only in the dense wet underbrush of the coniferous forests that parallel the northwestern coast. They are tiny, but overall size can be difficult to judge in the field. It is the very stubby, erect tail that is the **winter wren's** best mark. Also note the pronounced black-and-white barring on the sides just below the wing.

Mousy brown **house wrens** are numerous in woodlots and forest edges, as well as in residential areas. Although short, the barred tail is noticeably longer than that of the winter wren. There is some indistinct barring on the sides.

Bewick's wrens are numerous in the thickets and scrub underbrush of open woodlands, although they can also be found in fairly dense forest and chaparral.

There are ten subspecies of **Bewick's wren** in the West, varying slightly in size but significantly in shades of gray and brown. The white eyebrow is an easy mark; the outer tail feathers also show white.

54

Winter Wren

House Wren

Bewick's Wren

gray form

brown form

AMERICAN CROW

COMMON RAVEN

Chihuahuan ravens are slightly smaller relatives of the common raven that flock on southwestern grasslands.

Crows and their larger relatives, ravens, are the most intelligent North American birds. This is an opinion rooted in Native American folklore and confirmed by present-day ornithologists. Crows and ravens are not restricted to a specific diet but will take whatever is available. Their adaptability has permitted them to flourish. Crows are found everywhere except in deserts, mountain forests, and the Arctic. And ravens manage to live year-round even in northernmost Alaska.

Separating the larger **common raven** from the **American crow** is usually just a matter of estimating size and noting tail shape. The raven's wedge-shaped tail is usually easy to distinguish from the crow's blunt tail. Also note the heavier bill and shaggy neck. Their call is a hoarse, low-pitched c-r-ock.

Ravens are much more adept and acrobatic aerialists than crows, which are typically content to fly in the proverbial straight line.

Ornithologists officially recognize two crow species in the West, the American crow and the northwestern crow. The two species are virtually indistinguishable in the field. Those crows found on the Pacific coast from Puget Sound to Alaska are considered to be northwestern crows.

American &
Northwestern Crows

crow

raven

Common Raven

STELLER'S JAY

BLACK-BILLED MAGPIE

The yellow-billed magpie replaces the black-billed in much of central California. A bright yellow bill and eye patch are its most appreciable differences from the black-billed.

Steller's jay is numerous in conifers across the West, from coastal rain forests to the pine-oak woodlands of the arid Southwest. Nuts and seeds are staples where available, but like their close relatives, the crows, Steller's jays are omnivorous.

The dramatic crest on **Steller's jay** is an easy mark. Because it is largely sedentary, many local races have evolved with minor plumage differences. In some areas, the foreparts are evenly blackish; in others, there is contrast between portions of the head and back. Small streaks on the forehead and chin can be white, blue, or absent. Some birds have a small white crescent over the eye; a few also have a fleck below the eye. Young birds are duller, grayer.

The black-billed magpie is numerous in park-like areas — expanses of open ground dotted with large trees — and the thickets and groves along watercourses. It is usually seen in small, noisy flocks, often feeding on the ground. Insects and other invertebrates are its principal diet, but it also takes nuts, grains, and small animals, including roadkill.

There is more tail than bird to a **black-billed magpie,** and its color is a striking, iridescent green and blue. The black-and-white plumage pattern is almost as dramatic.

Steller's Jay

Black-billed Magpie

PINYON JAY

WESTERN SCRUB-JAY

In southeastern Arizona and the Big Bend area of Texas, the Mexican jay lives and behaves much like the western scrub-jay. It also looks much like a scrub-jay but lacks the distinctive throat markings and has a paler, less contrasting back patch.

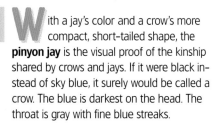

With a jay's color and a crow's more compact, short-tailed shape, the **pinyon jay** is the visual proof of the kinship shared by crows and jays. If it were black instead of sky blue, it surely would be called a crow. The blue is darkest on the head. The throat is gray with fine blue streaks.

Piñon nuts and other pine seeds are an important component of the pinyon jay's diet, and the birds are fairly numerous in western piñon-juniper highlands. In California, many are in ponderosa pine. In winter, some retreat to lowlands, including farms and suburbs. Pinyon jays fly like crows and live in large, noisy, crow-like flocks, except when nesting.

The scrub-jay is widespread and numerous in dense shrubbery, including that found in open woodlands and along streams. It is no stranger to suburbs and backyards, where it can become bold. Scrub-jays feed primarily on the ground, taking insects, small animals, and fallen nuts and seeds.

The intensity of the **western scrub-jay's** blues and grays varies regionally. All are lanky, long-tailed birds with gray-brown back patches. The white throat is streaked with blue-gray and bordered on the breast with a blue-gray necklace. Young birds are grayer than adults.

young

Pinyon Jay

Western Scrub-Jay

young

PARK

GRAY JAY

**CLARK'S
NUTCRACKER**

"Camp robber" is a
popular and very ap-
propriate name for
the brazen gray jay.
The name is also used
sometimes to refer to
Clark's nutcracker.

Common birds of western mountain conifers, the gray jay and Clark's nutcracker live all the way to the timberline. Gray jays are permanent residents, surviving winter with the help of cached foods. They manage to nest in late winter, enduring below-zero temperatures and having little or no fresh food (berries, bugs, and fungi are their staples). Forests that include spruce are preferred.

Gray jays have an unusually small bill for a jay. The dark area on the white head varies in extent and shade regionally. You seldom need to look for gray jays. If you are in one's range, it will often find you, gliding in on silent wings, alert for any food you might make available.

Clark's nutcracker feeds heavily on pine seeds, although it will happily take insects, berries, and other edibles. It caches many seeds for winter, using a large throat pouch to transport them. Many individuals leave subalpine areas for the lower slopes in winter, often gathering in good-sized, noisy flocks.

Very crow-like in shape, **Clark's nutcracker** also flies like a crow and often walks like one. It has a unique black-and-white wing and tail pattern that contrasts boldly with the pale gray body. Clark's nutcracker is a relatively tame bird, often attracted to humans.

62

young

Gray Jay

Clark's Nutcracker

GRAY BIRDS

TOWNSEND'S SOLITAIRE

MOCKINGBIRD

CATBIRD

Townsend's solitaire is fairly numerous in mountain conifers, from the lower slopes to the treeline in summer. It prefers relatively open areas that allow it to flycatch. Bugs are also taken from branches and the ground. In winter, it switches to a berry diet, juniper berries in particular, and is found primarily in juniper or piñon-juniper woodlands.

Fortunately, **Townsend's solitaire** often perches openly, allowing a good look. Its white eye-ring and long black tail are good marks. The wing markings and white outer tail feathers can be hard to see.

The familiar **mockingbird,** with the conspicuous white patches in its dark wings and tail, likes parklands and forest edges, where it can forage on the ground. Mockingbirds also pick fruit from bushes and trees. The only bird that much resembles a mockingbird is the loggerhead shrike (p. 42).

Catbirds are skulkers, usually hidden in brush, shrubs, and vine tangles. They are fairly numerous in early second-growth woods, streamside thickets, and brushy forest edges. Bugs and berries are their favorite foods.

The contrasting black cap and tail are the **catbird's** best marks. The rusty patch under the tail can be hard to see.

young

Townsend's
Solitaire

young

Mockingbird

Catbird

BLACK BIRDS

STARLING

RED-WINGED BLACKBIRD

There are now an estimated 200 million descendants of the approximately 100 starlings first imported from Europe and released in New York City's Central Park in the early 1890s.

Flocks of starlings are abundant in urban parks, suburban lawns, and farm fields, where they walk in search of seeds, grains, and a variety of animal life. Some live in relatively wild areas. They need woodlands to provide them with tree cavities in which to nest. Nest cavities are a limited resource, and the success of the starling comes at the expense of bluebirds and other native cavity nesters.

In all its varied plumages, the **starling's** very short tail and long, sharply pointed bill give it a distinct look. Winter birds are heavily spotted with white on the feather tips, which wear away to reveal a glossy black plumage by spring.

Although primarily a bird of marshes and fields, the abundant red-winged blackbird also lives in open woodlands, especially near water. Like starlings, they feed from the ground on a variety of items. Many also gather insects and seeds from marsh vegetation.

The brilliant shoulder patch of the male **red-winged blackbird** is often hidden when the bird is perched, and only the buff border is revealed. Female red-wings are smaller than males and suggest a large sparrow with a hint of red on the face and shoulder. The sexes often flock separately.

young

Starling

spring

fall

Red-winged Blackbird

young

BLACK BIRDS

BREWER'S BLACKBIRD

BROWN-HEADED COWBIRD

In much of Texas and Arizona, the bronzed cowbird shares habitat with the brown-headed cowbird.

Bronzed cowbirds are larger than the brown-headed and have heavier, longer bills and red eyes. Males lack the brown head; females are darker gray.

Brewer's blackbird is the most commonly seen blackbird in much of the West and can be found on farms, lawns, and parking lots, as well as in remote mountain woodlands, coastal beaches, and open fields.

Male **Brewer's blackbirds** have yellow eyes and glossy black plumage. In good light, a purplish sheen can be seen on the head, and sometimes there is a greenish sheen on the body. Females are gray-brown with dark eyes.

A good mark for the **brown-headed cowbird** is its conical bill, especially on the dull, gray-brown female. Males are black with a dark brown head that is not always obvious in poor light. (The bird is illustrated here rather than with other conically billed birds because it most resembles a blackbird.)

Cowbirds live and feed in open fields but use trees at the edges of woodlands or in fragmented woods for nesting and roosting. They are nest parasites. They lay their eggs in other birds' nests and abandon them to the care of the unwitting hosts. The host birds typically raise the cowbird chick, usually at the expense of their own young. Cowbirds once flocked with herds of buffalo (and were known as buffalo birds) but have now spread and multiplied until they have become serious pests.

68

♀ ♂ Brewer's Blackbird

Brown-headed Cowbird

♀

molting young
in fall

♂

ORIOLES

BULLOCK'S ORIOLE

HOODED ORIOLE

Although more brightly colored than blackbirds, orioles belong to the same family. The most telling similarity is the long, sharply pointed bill.

Orioles spend most of their time gleaning insects from trees and shrubs and are found in a variety of open deciduous woodlands, including suburban shade trees. Bullock's is the most numerous and widespread oriole in the West. Its nest, which can be conspicuous, is a large oval bag, often attached to the twigs on the outer branch of a large tree.

Male and female **Bullock's orioles** have different plumages. The adult male is bright and distinctive; note especially the large white wing patch. Females and yearling males lack the wing patch and the bright orange on the face and body. They are yellow to yellow-orange on the face, breast, and under the tail, blending to pale gray on the belly. The yearling male has a black throat and eye line.

Male **hooded orioles** vary from yellow to orange (and black, of course), with the darkest orange birds in Texas. Females and young males resemble their Bullock's oriole counterparts but are evenly colored below, not grayish on the belly. The slightly curved bill is a good mark.

Palm trees are favored by hooded orioles; their nests are often hidden in the tops. Ornamental plantings have allowed the birds to expand their range, and a few now overwinter. Males show buff bars on their black backs in winter.

Bullock's Oriole

yearling ♂

♀

♂

Hooded Oriole

yearling ♂

orange form
in winter

♂

♀

♂

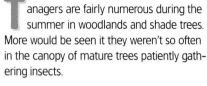

TANAGERS

Tanagers are fairly numerous during the summer in woodlands and shade trees. More would be seen if they weren't so often in the canopy of mature trees patiently gathering insects.

WESTERN TANAGER

The brilliant summer plumage of the male **western tanager** begins to turn to a female-like yellow-green dress by fall. His wings and tail remain black, however, not grayish like the female's. The female's plumage is much like that of female orioles, greenish yellow below and olive gray above, with two wing bars.

SUMMER TANAGER

Shape, especially bill shape, is the best mark separating female tanagers from orioles. The tanager is compact, its bill shorter and more swollen than the long pointed bill of the oriole.

Adult male **summer tanagers** are a rosy red year-round. Females are greenish or mustard and lack the wing bars of the female western tanager. Yearling males and some females show uneven reddish washes.

Hepatic tanagers are fairly numerous in the mountain forests in areas of the Southwest. Males resemble summer tanagers but have a gray cheek patch. Females have darker bills and grayer flanks than the female summer tanager.

Summer tanagers like woodland edges, streamsides, and scattered stands of trees. They take a variety of bugs but specialize in bees and wasps caught in flight or their grubs taken at the nest. They remove the stinger by wiping the dead insect against a branch.

72

Western Tanager

♂

♀

Summer Tanager

♂

yearling ♂

♀

VARIED THRUSH

ROBIN

Robins are members of the thrush family. They and varied thrushes are both birds of the forest floor and lower tree branches. Varied thrushes have not embraced civilization with the eagerness that robins have but are fairly numerous in the coniferous forest along the Pacific coast. Deep shade, dripping firs, and cool moss are their preferred surroundings. They feed on a variety of insects and also take many berries.

The orange underparts of the **varied thrush** suggest a robin, but even a casual glance reveals that there is something different about this "robin." The male's bold black markings and broad orange wing bars are obvious. They are repeated more subtly in gray-brown on the female.

Varied thrushes are shy, and robins in the wild are often shy also. Robins like open, sunny clearings and edges in mature forests, where they search for earthworms and bugs, just as they do in lawns. Berries supplement their diet, especially in cold weather.

Female **robins** are distinctively duller above and paler orange below than males. Their young are spotted below, like typical thrushes. Robins seen in a forest often appear particularly bright.

74

Varied Thrush

♂

♀

young

young

Robin

♂

SPOTTED THRUSHES

SWAINSON'S THRUSH

VEERY

HERMIT THRUSH

The spot-breasted thrushes are forest floor dwellers. Swainson's prefers riparian and wet coniferous forests, especially spruce; the veery is most numerous in moist deciduous second growth and shrubby areas. The hermit thrush occupies a variety of woodlands, dry and wet, coniferous and hardwood. It is the only spot-breasted thrush wintering in the US.

Back color and breast spotting are important marks for thrushes. The **veery's** back is an even tawny brown, and it has the least conspicuous breast spotting. **Swainson's** breast spots are more conspicuous, and its back and tail are darker (although coastal birds are rustier above than the interior form shown). Note the buff eye-ring and facial markings. Back color on **hermit thrushes** varies from gray-brown to olive brown. Most important, their tails are a contrasting rusty red. Hermit thrushes sometimes slowly pump their tails.

Thrushes are often heard singing. Swainson's gives an ascending swirl of flute-like notes described as *whip-poor-will-a-will-e-zee-zee-zee*. The veery is named for its song, a descending series that includes down-sliding *veer* or *vee-ur* notes. The hermit thrush's song has been described as *oh, holy-holy, ah, purity-purity, ehh, sweetly-sweetly,* ascending but less so than Swainson's.

Swainson's Thrush

Veery

Hermit Thrush

brown extreme

gray extreme

CHAT
BLUEBIRDS

CHAT

**MOUNTAIN
BLUEBIRD**

**WESTERN
BLUEBIRD**

Chats are skulkers best known for their song of jumbled squawks, whistles, and odd notes. Brush, shrubs, and vine tangles are their choice of habitat; bugs and berries, their favorite foods. They are also fairly numerous in early second-growth woods, streamside thickets, and brushy forest edges.

The **chat's** distinctive face pattern sets it apart from other birds with yellow breasts. The lores (areas between the white stripes) are black in the male, gray in the female.

Mountain bluebirds range from foothills to the treeline. They flycatch but more often perch or hover over open ground and flutter down to capture ground insects. Blue in the female **mountain bluebird** is limited to the rump, tail, and wings. Males are spectacularly blue.

The female **western bluebird** is also paler than her impressive mate, with bright blue only in her wings and tail. The blue is palest in young birds, which also have spotting on their backs and breasts. Family groups are often seen together throughout the summer in parks and suburbs.

Western bluebirds capture bugs on the ground, much as mountain bluebirds do. They are numerous and widespread except in deep forest and open areas lacking nest hole sites.

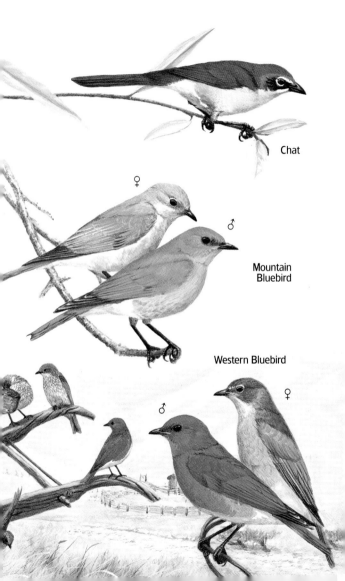

Chat

♀
♂

Mountain
Bluebird

Western Bluebird

♂
♀

RED-EYED VIREO

WARBLING VIREO

The vireos in this illustration and the next are easily confused with each other and some of the warblers that follow. Vireos have thicker bills than warblers. Most are also more deliberate, even sluggish, feeders than the typical active warbler. Be sure to check the bill shape of any plain or yellowish warbler-like bird; it might be a vireo.

Red-eyed and warbling vireos have pale eyebrows and plain wings; those in the next illustration have spectacles and wing bars. The eyebrow and bordering stripes of the **red-eyed vireo** are pronounced. There is also a notable contrast between the gray cap and the yellow-green hind neck and back. The red eye usually looks dark. On the **warbling vireo,** the eyebrow and eye line are dull; spring birds have little green on their backs or yellow on their sides, but fall birds are often brighter.

The red-eyed vireo and warbling vireo are numerous in western hardwood forests. However, both are birds of the treetops and often go unseen. They feed sluggishly on in-sects gleaned from foliage and are tireless singers. Red-eyed vireos sing a series of short robin-like phrases, such as *cherry-o-wit, cheree, sissy-a-wit, tee-oo.* Warbling vireos give a long, unbroken, drowsy warble.

80

Red-eyed Vireo

Warbling Vireo

fall

spring

HUTTON'S VIREO

CASSIN'S VIREO

PLUMBEOUS VIREO

The gray vireo is scarce in piñon-juniper. It has a fainter wing bar and eye-ring than the plumbeous vireo; its song is clearer and repeated faster.

Spectacles and wing bars distinguish Hutton's, Cassin's, and plumbeous vireos. The spectacles are a bold white in both the sober gray plumbeous and the more richly colored Cassin's. In Hutton's, they are off-white and less conspicuous. The portion of the spectacles ringing Hutton's eye is broken at the top.

Hutton's vireo can be mistaken for a kinglet (p. 98) or an empidonax flycatcher (p. 48), especially if the distinctive bill shape is not noted. Hutton's rarely flycatches; it gleans insects from foliage, much like a kinglet. Both wing bars are long in Hutton's, with the darkest spot on the wing between the wing bars, not below the lower one, as in the kinglet. Hutton's is fairly numerous in evergreen forests, especially live oaks.

Because their breeding ranges don't overlap, the white spectacles on a gray head are sure marks for both **Cassin's vireo** and the duller **plumbeous vireo** in summer. (Both were recently known as the solitary vireo.) Cassin's is fairly numerous in coniferous or mixed forests, especially moist areas. The plumbeous vireo prefers drier mountainous areas and is fairly numerous in stands of ponderosa pine and piñon-juniper. Songs of both birds are a series of short, gravelly phrases with long pauses.

ruby-crowned
kinglet p. 98

Hutton's Vireo

Cassin's Vireo

Plumbeous Vireo

YELLOW/ WING BARS

HERMIT WARBLER

TOWNSEND'S WARBLER

AUDUBON'S WARBLER

Grace's warbler is fairly numerous in the middle and upper levels of mountain pine forests in parts of the Southwest. It looks something like Audubon's but has a clear yellow throat, breast, and eyebrow.

In summer, hermit, Townsend's, and Audubon's warblers all gather insects in mature conifer forests. Audubon's is a generalist that forages at all levels and flycatches. It is the most common warbler in much of the West. Hermit and Townsend's warblers are specialists, gleaning bugs from the upper levels of dense forest, often unseen. They don't like forest edges, as Audubon's does.

In winter, Audubon's hunts berries and bugs in shrublands, suburbs, and varied forest types. Townsend's is sometimes seen in gardens in winter. It can live where temperatures stay above freezing and some insects survive. A few hermit warblers winter in coastal planted pines and live oak; most migrate farther south.

The bright yellow face and black throat would be easy marks for the **hermit warbler** if it weren't so often hidden in the forest canopy. **Townsend's warbler** is similar but more extensively yellow and has a black patch in the center of the yellow face. Females are duller than males in both species.

A yellow rump and side patch are reliable marks in all plumages of **Audubon's warbler.** Audubon's is now lumped with the similar myrtle warbler of the East into a species called the yellow-rumped warbler.

Hermit Warbler

♀

♂

Townsend's Warbler

spring ♂

young

Audubon's Warbler

spring ♂

spring ♀

ORANGE-CROWNED WARBLER

YELLOW WARBLER

Two of the most common and wide-spread warblers in the West are the orange-crowned and yellow warblers. Both forage for bugs in garden shrubs, woodland undergrowth, and areas of open scrub or early forest regeneration, especially moist areas and streamsides.

Orange-crowned and yellow warblers show yellow but have no wing bars. As in many warblers, the plumage of the **yellow warbler** varies with sex, age, and season. Spring adults are virtually all yellow — more so than any other warbler. Males are especially bright and have chestnut breast streaks.

A young yellow warbler in fall can be greenish and duller than some orange-crowned or Wilson's warblers (p. 88). On dull yellow warblers, look for the beady dark eye, the absence of a dark cap as in Wilson's, and for the yellow edges on the wing feathers that give their wings a striped effect. Another good mark is the yellow eye-ring, which becomes noticeable on dull birds. Often the yellow tail spots are visible.

Most **orange-crowned warblers** are non-descript olive-yellow birds (some are brighter) with only a thin broken eye-ring and a faint eye line. This plainness is, in fact, their best mark.

yellow
extreme

olive
extreme

Orange-crowned Warbler

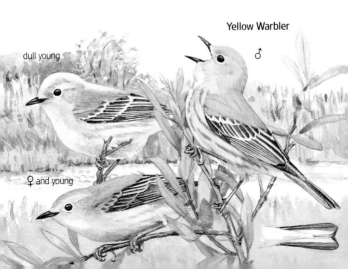

Yellow Warbler

♂

dull young

♀ and young

COMMON
YELLOWTHROAT

WILSON'S
WARBLER

The similar yellow warblers shown here and in the previous illustration can all be distinguished by call notes. The yellowthroat gives a hoarse *chuck;* Wilson's gives a dry *chep;* the orange-crowned's call note is a weak, metallic *tzit;* and the yelow warbler gives a sweet, musical *chip.*

Wilson's warbler and the yellowthroat show yellow and lack wing bars. Both are especially attracted to water. Wilson's is widespread and numerous in woodland shrubs and thickets. It is bold and active, picking bugs from foliage and often flycatching.

The yellowthroat is more secretive but is still often seen in the open. It forages at lower levels in brush and bushes and behaves a bit like a wren — very active, scolding, and then retreating into dense brush or briars. Marsh edges and boggy areas, wooded or not, are favorite nesting habitats.

Male **Wilson's warblers** and **common yellowthroats** are distinctively patterned. As with most warblers, it is the females and young birds that present identification problems. The crown of the female Wilson's is always dark, if not as black as the male's. Wilson's also has the distinctive habit of flicking its relatively long tail and holding it cocked expressively.

Young male yellowthroats show a hint of the adult male's black mask, but females don't. Her best plumage mark is a subtle one. Note how the yellow under the tail and on the breast blends to a brownish gray on the belly. Similar warblers are yellow from breast to tail.

88

Common Yellowthroat

♂

♀

young ♂

Wilson's Warbler

♀

♂

YELLOW/ NO BARS

VIRGINIA'S WARBLER

NASHVILLE WARBLER

MACGILLIVRAY'S WARBLER

A few Nashville warblers remain throughout the winter in coastal California woodlands.

The drabbest of the gray-headed warblers, Virginia's is fairly numerous in dense scrub and small trees on steep slopes, usually at mid-elevations. It is sometimes in streamside willows. The bright yellow on the rump and under the tail is a good mark for **Virginia's warbler**. The white eye-ring is prominent, but the chestnut crown patch is usually concealed. Males have a wash of lemon yellow on the breast that is reduced in females and absent in young birds.

The **Nashville warbler** is a brighter version of Virginia's warbler, yellow below and greenish above with a white eye-ring bold against the gray head. Females are a little duller. They like open deciduous or mixed woods, preferably second growth and with much undergrowth. Fairly numerous, they are a relatively easy warbler to see as they scour the outer leaves of trees for bugs.

MacGillivray's warbler is usually difficult to sight. It is fairly numerous but likes denser forest (coniferous or mixed) than the Nashville warbler and usually hunts insects on or close to the ground in streamside thickets or thick underbrush. The gray hood and broken white eye-ring of the male **MacGillivray's warbler** are sure marks. Hoods on females and young birds are noticeably paler. The pink legs often show prominently.

90

young

Virginia's
Warbler

♂

Nashville Warbler

♀ MacGillivray's Warbler

♂

young

AMERICAN REDSTART

BLACK-THROATED GRAY WARBLER

NORTHERN WATERTHRUSH

The flame-like flash in the black wings and tail of the male **American redstart** is a dazzling mark (females are gray with yellow flashes). Redstarts feed actively and often flycatch acrobatically, making them easy to see and identify. Unfortunately, they are scarce in the West, best seen in deciduous growth near water.

Black-throated gray warblers are fairly numerous in the West and are easy to sight, although not as ostentatious as the redstart. They forage openly and deliberately in the foliage of shrubs and trees for insects. Piñon-juniper woodlands are a favorite habitat, but they can be found in many open coniferous or mixed woodlands with heavy undergrowth. The black-and-white head pattern (gray-and-white in females and young) is an easy mark for the **black-throated gray warbler.**

Waterthrushes are warblers, not thrushes, that feed primarily on the ground. They often wade in cool western bogs and wooded wetlands while scouring floating debris and banks for insects. In the western US, they are scarce and usually out of sight. When walking, they continually bob their bodies and wag their tails distinctively. The broad eyebrow and dark breast streaks are good plumage marks for the **northern waterthrush.**

American
Redstart

Black-throated Gray Warbler

♂

young

♀

Northern Waterthrush

CHICKADEES

BLACK-CAPPED CHICKADEE

CHESTNUT-BACKED CHICKADEE

MOUNTAIN CHICKADEE

The boreal chickadee lives in the Canadian Rockies and Cascades. It is similar to the black-backed but has a brownish cap and back and rusty buff sides.

Chickadees are much alike, bold little birds known to sometimes alight on hunters or others who sit quietly in the woods. Except when nesting, they are usually in small flocks.

In summer, they feed heavily on insects gleaned from twigs, limbs, and tree trunks. In fall, when bugs and larvae become hard to find and the year's crop of seeds and nuts ripens, chickadees adapt to the new bounty. Many visit backyards to feed on sunflower seeds set out for them. They often carefully store seeds under loose bark or in crevices along a limb. Each species is numerous but keeps mostly to its own habitat in summer.

The **black-capped chickadee,** with its familiar black-and-white head, is the most widespread of the group. It is found in a variety of deciduous or mixed forest habitats, from scattered trees to forest interior.

Chestnut-backed chickadees favor the dense coastal rain forest and streamside woods. California birds have gray sides with little or no chestnut.

Coniferous forests of the interior mountains — up to 10,000 feet high — are home to the **mountain chickadee.** The white eyebrow is an easy mark. The form in the Rockies has buff tinges on its back and sides.

Black-capped Chickadee

Chestnut-backed Chickadee

Mountain Chickadee

BUSHTIT

OAK & JUNIPER TITMICE

WRENTIT

The bridled titmouse is numerous in oaks and cottonwoods in the mountains and foothills of parts of Arizona. It combines the crest of a titmouse with black-and-white face markings suggesting a chickadee.

Small, twittering flocks of bushtits are numerous over most of the year in piñon-juniper, live oak, chaparral, riparian areas, and suburbs. Friendly, bold, and chickadee-like, they glean insects from vegetation. **Bushtits** are small, long-tailed, gray-brown birds. Coastal birds have brownish caps. Some southern interior males have a black face patch. Females differ from males by having a pale eye.

Perky crests distinguish the plain gray **titmice.** Coastal birds are a little browner and shorter-billed than interior ones. The two have only recently achieved species status. Oak titmice are named for the oak and mixed woodlands they inhabit. The juniper titmice of the interior live in piñon-juniper woodlands. Titmice feed and behave much like their close kin, the chickadees.

Wrentits are numerous in dense brush, where they glean insects from the bark and twigs. They are found in brushy streamsides or forest edges and especially in chaparral. Neither wren nor tit, they suggest both, being active and noisy but secretive. The male doesn't even show himself to sing his ringing, staccato song: *yip, yip, yip,* accelerating to a barely descending, "bouncing-ball" trill. The long tail is a good mark. The form illustrated is typical of northern **wrentits.** Southern California birds are paler below and less distinctly streaked.

black-eared form

coastal ♂

inerior ♂

Bushtit

♀

Oak & Juniper
Titmice

Wrentit

GNATCATCHER & KINGLETS

RUBY-CROWNED KINGLET

GOLDEN-CROWNED KINGLET

BLUE-GRAY GNATCATCHER

The tiny kinglets and gnatcatchers are closely related in spite of their different shapes. Kinglets nest in conifers and are numerous in a wide variety of woodlands in winter and during migration. They feed from just above the ground to the treetops. The ruby-crowned kinglet takes a few seeds in winter, but kinglets manage to find hidden larvae and insect matter even in cold and snowy weather.

The color of its crown and the white eyebrow are good marks for the **golden-crowned kinglet. Ruby-crowned kinglets** are more nondescript; only the male shows red, and it is usually concealed. The tiny bill, plump body, short tail, and wing-flicking habit give the ruby-crowned a different look from the warblers with which it might be confused. The clinching marks are a white eye-ring broken at the top and a white wing bar bordered below by a dark patch — the kinglet patch.

The **blue-gray gnatcatcher** suggests a very small mockingbird — long, slender, and very active. It often cocks its long tail expressively, flashing the white underside. Both sexes have a white eye-ring; males have a narrow black eyebrow and a blue-gray crown. Gnatcatchers pick bugs from leaves and snatch some in flight. They are fairly numerous in deciduous trees and shrubs and in piñon-juniper woods.

Ruby-crowned Kinglet

♀

♂

Golden-crowned
Kinglet

♀

♂

Blue-gray Gnatcatcher

♀

summer ♂

GREEN-TAILED TOWHEE

CALIFORNIA TOWHEE

SPOTTED TOWHEE

Canyon towhees are fairly numerous in parts of the Southwest. A necklace of fine dark streaks and a rusty crown patch distinguish them from California towhees.

owhees are shy ground dwellers that scratch a living out of the seeds and insects in leaf litter and on shrubs. They are often easier heard than seen.

Green-tailed towhees avoid typical forest, but trees are often interspersed in the scrub they prefer. They are also fairly numerous in burns, clear-cuts, and other disturbed patches in forests. The green in the wings and tail of the **green-tailed towhee** is noticeable only in good light. The dull rusty cap is a good mark, as are the white throat and gray whisker.

California towhees are numerous on chaparral-covered slopes. Brushy forest edges and back-yard shrubs are also favored. Around farms and in the suburbs, a piece of farm equipment or parked car can substitute for brush. There are no prominent plumage marks for the **California towhee.** It's a big gray-brown finch with some rusty orange under its tail.

With its dark hood and rusty sides, the **spotted towhee** is the best marked of the clan. There is some regional variation in the color of the back and the amount of spotting. Females are always paler than males. The spotted towhee exploits brushy habitats from coastal lowlands through the foothills of western mountains and into the northern Great Plains.

Green-tailed Towhee

California Towhee

Spotted Towhee

♂

♀

GROSBEAKS

BLACK-HEADED GROSBEAK

EVENING GROSBEAK

Big finches with very heavy bills, the grosbeaks are woodland birds that are prize visitors to backyard feeders. Black-headed grosbeaks spend most of their time in a wide variety of open woodlands. They are fairly numerous and eat insects as much as seeds in summer.

Adult male **black-headed grosbeaks** are a striking butterscotch and black that is easy to identify. Also note the white patches in the wings. The female's plumage resembles that of many smaller finches, but her large bill, wash of buff yellow on the breast, and distinct eyebrow and crown stripes are good marks. There is some fine streaking below, mainly along the sides. Both male and female show yellow in the underwing in flight. Young birds resemble females.

Evening grosbeaks are relatively tame birds that live in mountain conifers and mixed woods, feeding on seeds and buds. Flocks of evening grosbeaks visit feeders in winter.

The male **evening grosbeak** is as distinctive as the male black-headed. The large white wing patches, stubby tail, and yellow forehead and eyebrows are all easily seen marks. Females are much grayer and have smaller white wing patches.

102

Black-headed
Grosbeak

♂

♀

Evening Grosbeak

♂

♀

GOLD-FINCHES

AMERICAN GOLDFINCH

LAWRENCE'S GOLDFINCH

Goldfinches use scattered trees and forest edges for shelter and nesting. They spend most of their time in weedy fields gathering seeds, which they eat almost exclusively. Flocks of goldfinches can be recognized by their distinctive roller-coaster flight.

American goldfinches are abundant and feed heavily on the seeds of thistles and dandelions. The male **American goldfinch** in summer is the only yellow bird — a stunning lemon yellow — with black wings and tail. Female American goldfinches and males in fall and winter are a dull, unstreaked olive brown above. The combination of white wing bars and white under the tail is a good mark. Males retain their black wings and tail in winter and also a small but bright yellow shoulder patch.

The range of Lawrence's goldfinch is much more restricted than that of the American goldfinch. Lawrence's is erratic in its wanderings — common in an area one year, rare the next. Dry areas are its favorite haunts. The yellow on **Lawrence's goldfinch** is more restricted than in other goldfinches, just a wash on the breast and rump and a bright flash in the wings. The overall body color is gray, browner in winter. Males have a distinctive black face.

summer ♀

summer ♂

winter ♂

American Goldfinch

American

Lawrence's

Lawrence's Goldfinch

summer ♀

summer ♂

winter ♂

LAZULI BUNTING

PINE SISKIN

LESSER GOLDFINCH

The indigo bunting and blue grosbeak can be found in parts of the Southwest and California. The males of both are deep blue-black overall except for brown wing bars on the grosbeak.

Lazuli buntings are fairly numerous in brush and shrubs from coastal tangles to arid scrub, including brushy woodlands and disturbed forest. They are seed-eaters but also take berries and, in summer, many insects. In color and pattern, **lazuli buntings** suggest western bluebirds (p. 78). The stubby, conical bill and white wing bars of the bunting are good distinguishing marks. The blue on some females can easily go unobserved. Without streaks or notable pattern, plainness is her best mark.

Streaks are one of the **pine siskin's** best marks. The only gold this goldfinch has is in the wings and tail, and it's obvious only in flight. Like goldfinches, siskins bound along in undulating flight. They are numerous in open coniferous forests. Insects and small seeds are taken from ground level to the treetops.

There are two forms of the **lesser goldfinch** in the US. Males in the coastal states have green or mostly green backs. Black-backed males become increasingly common to the east. Females can be reliably separated from female American goldfinches (p. 104) by the yellow (not white) under the tail. Lesser goldfinches have much the same food and habitat preferences of the American goldfinch but also occur in drier areas.

106

Lazuli Bunting ♀ ♂

Pine Siskin

Lesser Goldfinch

black-backed ♂

♀

green-backed ♂

CROSSBILL & FINCH

RED CROSSBILL

HOUSE FINCH

Two other large red finches wander in flocks in some high western conifer forests. The white-winged crossbill resembles the red crossbill but has broad white wing bars.

Male pine grosbeaks are rosy red with narrow white wing bars; the female, gray with an olive head and rump.

Red crossbills are conifer seed specialists and are fairly numerous in mature, cone-bearing conifers of western mountains. They wander in flocks, and where food abounds, they nest. Their unusual bills are adapted to extract seeds from cones. The bird typically holds a pine cone in one foot as it pries each scale open with its bill, exposing the seed at the base to a swipe of its tongue.

The cones of different conifers vary, as do the size and bill shape of the crossbills that feed on them. Six types are known in the West; all have very similar plumage. Most male **red crossbills** have brick-red bodies, but some are reddish yellow and even greenish. Females are grayish olive with greenish or greenish yellow tints on the breast and rump.

House finches are abundant on developed land. They are also numerous in forest edges and open coniferous forests below about 6,000 feet. Weed seeds are a major food.

The best mark distinguishing the male **house finch** from the similar Cassin's and purple finches (p. 110) is the distinct brown streaking on its sides and belly. The red color varies to orange and yellow. The face of the female house finch is plain; her breast streaks are fine and extend all the way under her tail.

108

young

Red Crossbill ♂

♀

♀

House Finch

♂

RED FINCHES

CASSIN'S FINCH

PURPLE FINCH

Rosy-finches are fairly numerous in some alpine areas near snowbanks. They are dark, ranging from brown to blackish, with contrasting white underwings noticeable in flight. Males have pink on their wings and bellies. Some have distinctive gray areas on their crowns.

Cassin's finch and the purple finch are difficult, at first, to separate from each other and from house finches (p. 108). The only easy part is separating males from females. House finches are by far the most abundant of the three in developed areas.

Only the male house finch has brown belly steaks. Male **Cassin's** and **purple finches** have blurry, reddish side streaks at most. Cassin's has its red concentrated on the top and front of the crown; the hind crown and nape are predominantly brown. On the male purple finch, the red extends to the hind crown, nape, and back and tends to be more raspberry. (In the house finch, the red areas include a U-shaped band on the forehead and eyebrows.)

The contrast of the broad white eyebrow and whisker stripe on the female purple finch is her best mark. The stripes can also be seen clearly in shades of red on the male. The face of the female house finch is much plainer, and Cassin's is intermediate.

Purple finches are widespread in winter. In summer, they are most common in moist coniferous and mixed forests. Cassin's nests in interior mountain conifers, at higher elevations than the purple in places where the ranges overlap. Both are seed-eaters that also take buds and berries.

Cassin's Finch

♀   ♂

Purple Finch

♂   ♀

JUNCOS

SLATE-COLORED JUNCO

GRAY-HEADED JUNCO

OREGON JUNCO

The white-winged junco inhabits the ponderosa pines of the Black Hills, South Dakota, and adjoining Wyoming and Montana. It has white wing bars. Otherwise it looks much like the slate-colored junco.

Scientists have often reversed themselves on whether the different juncos should be classified as species or as races of a single species. Currently all forms are grouped as one species: the dark-eyed junco. They are abundant in open woods, forest edges, and clearings.

All forms of the dark-eyed junco have dark eyes, pale bills, and white outer tail feathers. The white in the tail is especially conspicuous when the bird is disturbed while feeding on the ground and flies to a low tree branch.

The **slate-colored junco** is relatively scarce and seen only during winter and migration in most of the West. Males are slate gray with white bellies. Females are duller, browner, and can show contrast between the hood and the back.

The **gray-headed junco** of the Rockies and Great Basin has a pale gray head and sides and a rusty-colored back.

The **Oregon junco** is the most numerous form in the Pacific Coast states. The male has a black hood, buff to pinkish sides, and a rusty brown back. Females are duller. In the northern Rockies, Oregon juncos have broader pink sides and a paler hood with a contrasting dark area in front of the eye.

112

♀
♂
Slate-colored
Junco

Gray-headed Junco

♀
Oregon
Junco

Oregon pink-
sided junco

CROWNED SPARROWS

GOLDEN-CROWNED SPARROW

WHITE-CROWNED SPARROW

In both golden- and white-crowned sparrows, the young birds just out of the nest have streaked breasts. The streaks don't last long, perhaps a few weeks at most.

Prominent crown stripes distinguish the golden-crowned and white-crowned sparrows. Both are abundant in winter and may flock and feed together in a variety of grass, scrub, or bare-ground habitats, often near residential areas. The white-crowns that nest in the US are often in alpine thickets, clear-cuts, and coastal scrub.

Both **golden-** and **white-crowned sparrows** are large for sparrows. The golden-crowned is slightly larger and has duskier underparts. In the white-crowned sparrow, the bill is pink to orange. In the golden-crowned, the upper mandible is dusky; the lower one, pale. These minor points can be useful in identifying some young birds in a mixed flock.

Young birds are not as readily identifiable as the unmistakable adults. Young golden-crowns usually show at least a hint of the adult's crown pattern and color (on the forehead), but it requires imagination to see it at times. Young white-crowned sparrows have brown crown stripes.

Gambel's form of the white-crowned is the most common subspecies in many areas. Its black eye line stops at the eye instead of continuing in front to the bill. Some coastal birds are browner than those shown.

114

Golden-crowned Sparrow

young

very young late summer

White-crowned Sparrow

Gambel's form

young

very young late summer

LARK SPARROW

CHIPPING SPARROW

Over parts of the West, chipping sparrows are replaced by tree sparrows in winter.

The tree sparrow has a rusty cap and gray underparts like the chippie, but lacks the black eye line and has a prominent breast spot like the lark sparrow's.

Lark sparrows are primarily ground feeders that dwell on prairies, brushy pastures, and similar open lands, sometimes grassy areas with scattered trees. Small flocks feed together even in nesting season, taking mostly seeds and some bugs.

In flight, the white corners in the tail are prominent and a particularly good mark for the **lark sparrow.** The distinctive face markings and black center spot on its clear breast are easy marks for perched birds. Young birds are much plainer but always show a dull version of the adult's face pattern.

Chipping sparrows are largely ground-feeding sparrows but almost always choose areas with trees, especially conifers. They are numerous in mountain meadows and grassy openings in coniferous and oak forests. Except when nesting, they forage in small flocks, typically gathering in trees around a feeding area before descending, one after the other, to the ground.

The rusty cap, white eyebrow, and black eye line are a good set of marks for the gray-breasted **chipping sparrow** in summer. The face and crown are duller in winter, especially on first-winter birds. Young birds hold their breast streaks until well into fall.

Lark Sparrow

young

Chipping Sparrow

1st winter

young

summer

SPARROWS

SONG SPARROW

LINCOLN'S SPARROW

FOX SPARROW

Song, Lincoln's, and fox sparrows all usually forage alone, not in flocks. They eat insects in summer, as well as seeds.

Song and Lincoln's sparrows are similar and closely related but react quite differently to humans. The abundant song sparrow adapts to people easily and will nest near houses. It accepts a wide variety of brush and shrub habitat, from lowland marshes to dry upland fencerows; most prefer water and woods nearby. Lincoln's sparrow is shy and nests in wilderness, usually open, boggy areas with willows, alders, or other dense shrubs. It often sings from a tall tree at a bog's edge.

The **song sparrow** is noted for the central spot on its streaked breast, but it shares that feature with the fox sparrow and sometimes Lincoln's. Note the heavy, dark whisker stripes as well. **Lincoln's sparrow** has a finer whisker stripe and breast streaking, but its best mark is the buff base color on the breast and above the whisker stripe.

Fox sparrows are heavily streaked below and have a central breast spot like song sparrows. The large amount of plumage variation makes some individuals difficult to identify, but **fox sparrows** are larger than song sparrrows and have distinctive square-tipped reddish tails. The song sparrow has a long rounded tail. Fox sparrows are fairly numerous but furtive in the underbrush at woodland edges or streamside, foraging in leaf litter or dense chaparral.

Song Sparrow

Lincoln's Sparrow

Fox Sparrow

regional
variations

CHECK-LIST AND INDEX

How many species of birds have you identified? Keeping a record is the only way to know. Sooner or later, even the most casual bird-watcher makes notes of the species seen on a trip or in a day. People keep backyard lists, year lists, state and provincial lists, every kind of checklist. All serious birders maintain a life list. Seeing your life list grow can become part of the pleasure of bird-watching. The pages that follow are designed to serve as your checklist of western trailside songbirds as well as an index to their illustrations in this guide.

English names used in this guide and listed in the index are the familiar names used in common conversation. For the most part, they are the same as the formal English names adopted by the American Ornithologists' Union in the seventh edition of their *Check-list of North American Birds,* 1998.

When the formal AOU English name differs from the common name used in this guide, the AOU English name is given on the second line of the index entry. The Latin names in italics are the AOU's scientific names.

✓ Species		Date	Location

BREWER'S BLACKBIRD   68
Euphagus cyanocephalus

RED-WINGED BLACKBIRD   66
Agelaius phoeniceus

MOUNTAIN BLUEBIRD   78
Sialia currucoides

WESTERN BLUEBIRD   78
Sialia mexicana

LAZULI BUNTING   106
Passerina amoena

BUSHTIT   96
Psaltriparus minimus

CATBIRD   64
Gray Catbird
Dumetella carolinensis

CHAT   78
Yellow-breasted Chat
Icteria virens

BLACK-CAPPED CHICKADEE 94
Poecile atricapillus

CHESTNUT-BACKED CHICKADEE 94
Poecile rufescens

MOUNTAIN CHICKADEE   94
Poecile gambeli

BROWN-HEADED COWBIRD 68
Molothrus ater

BROWN CREEPER   40
Certhia americana

RED CROSSBILL   108
Loxia curvirostra

AMERICAN CROW   56
Corvus brachyrhynchos

CASSIN'S FINCH   110
Carpodacus cassinii

✓ **Species**		**Date**	**Location**
○ HOUSE FINCH *Carpodacus mexicanus*	108	....	....
○ PURPLE FINCH *Carpodacus purpureus*	110	....	....
○ RED-SHAFTED FLICKER Northern Flicker *Colaptes auratus*	32	....	....
○ ASH-THROATED FLYCATCHER *Myiarchus cinerascens*	46	....	....
○ EMPIDONAX FLYCATCHERS genus *Empidonax*	48	....	....
○ OLIVE-SIDED FLYCATCHER *Contopus cooperi*	48	....	....
○ VERMILION FLYCATCHER *Pyrocephalus rubinus*	50	....	....
○ BLUE-GRAY GNATCATCHER *Polioptila caerulea*	98	....	....
○ AMERICAN GOLDFINCH *Carduelis tristis*	104	....	....
○ LAWRENCE'S GOLDFINCH *Carduelis lawrencei*	104	....	....
○ LESSER GOLDFINCH *Carduelis psaltria*	106	....	....
○ BLACK-HEADED GROSBEAK *Pheucticus melanocephalus*	102	....	....
○ EVENING GROSBEAK *Coccothraustes vespertinus*	102	....	....
○ ALLEN'S HUMMINGBIRD *Selasphorus sasin*	28	....	....
○ ANNA'S HUMMINGBIRD *Calypte anna*	30	....	....
○ BLACK-CHINNED HUMMINGBIRD *Archilochus alexandri*	30	....	....
○ BROAD-TAILED HUMMINGBIRD *Selasphorus platycercus*	30	....	....

✓	Species		Date	Location

			Date	Location
○	**CALLIOPE HUMMINGBIRD** *Stellula calliope*	30	....	....
○	**RUFOUS HUMMINGBIRD** *Selasphorus rufus*	28	....	....
○	**GRAY JAY** *Perisoreus canadensis*	62	....	....
○	**PINYON JAY** *Gymnorhinus cyanocephalus*	60	....	....
○	**STELLER'S JAY** *Cyanocitta stelleri*	58	....	....
○	**DARK-EYED JUNCO** *Junco hyemalis*	112	....	....
○	**CASSIN'S KINGBIRD** *Tyrannus vociferans*	44	....	....
○	**EASTERN KINGBIRD** *Tyrannus tyrannus*	46	....	....
○	**WESTERN KINGBIRD** *Tyrannus verticalis*	44	....	....
○	**GOLDEN-CROWNED KINGLET** *Regulus satrapa*	98	....	....
○	**RUBY-CROWNED KINGLET** *Regulus calendula*	98	....	....
○	**BLACK-BILLED MAGPIE** *Pica pica*	58	....	....
○	**MOCKINGBIRD** Northern Mockingbird *Mimus polyglottos*	64	....	....
○	**CLARK'S NUTCRACKER** *Nucifraga columbiana*	62	....	....
○	**RED-BREASTED NUTHATCH** *Sitta canadensis*	40	....	....
○	**WHITE-BREASTED NUTHATCH** *Sitta carolinensis*	40	....	....
○	**BULLOCK'S ORIOLE** *Icterus bullockii*	70	....	....

✓ Species		Date	Location
○ HOODED ORIOLE *Icterus cucullatus*	70	....	
○ BLACK PHOEBE *Sayornis nigricans*	50	....	
○ COMMON RAVEN *Corvus corax*	56	....	
○ AMERICAN REDSTART *Setophaga ruticilla*	92	....	
○ ROBIN American Robin *Turdus migratorius*	74	....	
○ RED-BREASTED SAPSUCKER *Sphyrapicus ruber*	38	....	
○ RED-NAPED SAPSUCKER *Sphyrapicus nuchalis*	38	....	
○ WILLIAMSON'S SAPSUCKER *Sphyrapicus thyroideus*	38	....	
○ WESTERN SCRUB-JAY *Aphelocoma californica*	60	....	
○ LOGGERHEAD SHRIKE *Lanius ludovicianus*	42	....	
○ PINE SISKIN *Carduelis pinus*	106	....	
○ TOWNSEND'S SOLITAIRE *Myadestes townsendi*	64	....	
○ CHIPPING SPARROW *Spizella passerina*	116	....	
○ FOX SPARROW *Passerella iliaca*	118	....	
○ GOLDEN-CROWNED SPARROW *Zonotrichia atricapilla*	114	....	
○ LARK SPARROW *Chondestes grammacus*	116	....	
○ LINCOLN'S SPARROW *Melospiza lincolnii*	118	....	

✓ Species		Date	Location
○ SONG SPARROW *Melospiza melodia*	118		
○ WHITE-CROWNED SPARROW *Zonotrichia leucophrys*	114		
○ STARLING European Starling *Sturnus vulgaris*	66		
○ ROUGH-WINGED SWALLOW Northern Rough-winged Swallow *Stelgidopteryx serripennis*	26		
○ TREE SWALLOW *Tachycineta bicolor*	26		
○ VIOLET-GREEN SWALLOW *Tachycineta thalassina*	26		
○ VAUX'S SWIFT *Chaetura vauxi*	24		
○ WHITE-THROATED SWIFT *Aeronautes saxatalis*	24		
○ SUMMER TANAGER *Piranga rubra*	72		
○ WESTERN TANAGER *Piranga ludoviciana*	72		
○ CALIFORNIA THRASHER *Toxostoma redivivum*	52		
○ HERMIT THRUSH *Catharus guttatus*	76		
○ SWAINSON'S THRUSH *Catharus ustulatus*	76		
○ VARIED THRUSH *Ixoreus naevius*	74		
○ OAK TITMOUSE *Baeolophus inornatus*	96		
○ JUNIPER TITMOUSE *Baeolophus griseus*	96		
○ CALIFORNIA TOWHEE *Pipilo crissalis*	100		

✓ Species		Date	Location

	Species		Date	Location
○	GREEN-TAILED TOWHEE *Pipilo chlorurus*	100	....	....
○	SPOTTED TOWHEE *Pipilo maculatus*	100	....	....
○	VEERY *Catharus fuscescens*	76	....	....
○	CASSIN'S VIREO *Vireo cassinii*	82	....	....
○	HUTTON'S VIREO *Vireo huttoni*	82	....	....
○	PLUMBEOUS VIREO *Vireo plumbeus*	82	....	....
○	RED-EYED VIREO *Vireo olivaceus*	80	....	....
○	WARBLING VIREO *Vireo gilvus*	80	....	....
○	AUDUBON'S WARBLER Yellow-rumped Warbler *Dendroica coronata*	84	....	....
○	BLACK-THROATED GRAY WARBLER *Dendroica nigrescens*	92	....	....
○	HERMIT WARBLER *Dendroica occidentalis*	84	....	....
○	MACGILLIVRAY'S WARBLER *Oporornis tolmiei*	90	....	....
○	NASHVILLE WARBLER *Vermivora ruficapilla*	90	....	....
○	ORANGE-CROWNED WARBLER *Vermivora celata*	86	....	....
○	TOWNSEND'S WARBLER *Dendroica townsendi*	84	....	....
○	VIRGINIA'S WARBLER *Vermivora virginiae*	90	....	....
○	WILSON'S WARBLER *Wilsonia pusilla*	88	....	....

✓ Species		Date	Location
○ YELLOW WARBLER *Dendroica petechia*	86	....	....
○ NORTHERN WATERTHRUSH *Seiurus noveboracensis*	92	....	....
○ CEDAR WAXWING *Bombycilla cedrorum*	42	....	....
○ ACORN WOODPECKER *Melanerpes formicivorus*	36	....	....
○ DOWNY WOODPECKER *Picoides pubescens*	34	....	....
○ HAIRY WOODPECKER *Picoides villosus*	34	....	....
○ LADDER-BACKED WOODPECKER *Picoides scalaris*	36	....	....
○ NUTTALL'S WOODPECKER *Picoides nuttallii*	36	....	....
○ PILEATED WOODPECKER *Dryocopus pileatus*	32	....	....
○ WESTERN WOOD-PEWEE *Contopus sordidulus*	48	....	....
○ BEWICK'S WREN *Thryomanes bewickii*	54	....	....
○ CANYON WREN *Catherpes mexicanus*	52	....	....
○ HOUSE WREN *Troglodytes aedon*	54	....	....
○ ROCK WREN *Salpinctes obsoletus*	52	....	....
○ WINTER WREN *Troglodytes troglodytes*	54	....	....
○ WRENTIT *Chamaea fasciata*	96	....	....
○ COMMON YELLOWTHROAT *Geothlypis trichas*	88	....	....

Want to Help Conserve Birds?

It's as Easy as ABC!

By becoming a member of the American
Bird Conservancy, you can help ensure
work is being done to protect many of the
species in this field guide. You can receive *Bird
Conservation* magazine quarterly to learn about bird
conservation throughout the Americas and *World Birdwatch*
magazine for information on international bird conservation.

Make a difference to birds.
Copy this card and mail to the address listed below.

❏ **Yes,** I want to become a member and receive *Bird
Conservation* magazine.
A check in the amount of $18 is enclosed.

❏ **Yes,** I want to become an International member of
ABC and receive both *Bird Conservation* and
World Birdwatch magazines.
A check in the amount of $40 is enclosed.

NAME

ADDRESS

CITY/STATE/ZIP CODE

Return to: American Bird Conservancy
1250 24th Street NW, Suite 400; Washington, DC 20037
or call **1-888-BIRD-MAG** or e-mail: abc@abcbirds.org

Memberships are tax deductible to the extent allowable by law.